BRIGHT
IDEA
BOOKS

ANCIENT
Aliens

by Meg Gaertner

CAPSTONE PRESS
a capstone imprint

Bright Idea Books are published by Capstone Press
1710 Roe Crest Drive, North Mankato, Minnesota 56003
www.mycapstone.com

Library of Congress Cataloging-in-Publication Data
Names: Gaertner, Meg, author.
Title: Ancient aliens / by Meg Gaertner.
Description: North Mankato, Minnesota : Capstone Press, [2020] | Series:
  Aliens | Includes bibliographical references and index. | Audience: Grade
  4 to 6.
Identifiers: LCCN 2018058402 (print) | LCCN 2018060260 (ebook) | ISBN
  9781543571134 (ebook) | ISBN 9781543571059 (hardcover) | ISBN
  9781543574920 (pbk.)
Subjects: LCSH: Civilization, Ancient--Extraterrestrial influences--Juvenile
  literature. | Extraterrestrial beings--Juvenile literature.
Classification: LCC CB156 (ebook) | LCC CB156 .G324 2020 (print) | DDC
  001.94--dc23
LC record available at https://lccn.loc.gov/2018058402

All internet sites appearing in back matter were available and accurate when this book was sent to press.

Editorial Credits
Editor: Claire Vanden Branden
Designer: Becky Daum
Production Specialist: Ryan Gale

Photo Credits
Alamy: ClassicStock, 22; iStockphoto: PeskyMonkey, 5, Adrian Wojcik, 21, Fat Camera, 30–31, Matjaz Slanic, 9, Starcevic, 6–7; Newscom: Album/Prisma, 18; Shutterstock Images: Abbie Warnock-Matthews, 13, Anthony Booker, 25, 28, dmitry_islentev, 14–15, Dotted Yeti, cover (spaceship), Fred Mantel, 26–27, mountainpix, 17, Skreidzeleu, cover (pyramid), Yulliii, 10–11

Design Elements: Shutterstock Images, Red Line Editorial

Printed in the United States of America.
PA70

TABLE OF CONTENTS

CHAPTER 1

ANCIENT ALIEN
Theory

People look to the sky. They think about **alien** life. Are aliens real? Will they visit Earth one day?

Some people say aliens are real. They have already been to Earth. They have visited many times. This is the **ancient** alien **theory**.

Stonehenge is a group of rocks in England. Ancient alien believers think aliens helped people build this structure. Scientists disagree.

SHAPING HISTORY

This idea says aliens shaped human history. It says they came to Earth in ancient times. They helped people build cities. They gave people new tools.

Teotihuacan is a city in Mexico. Ancient alien believers think it was built with the help of aliens.

ALIENS VS. DINOSAURS

Dinosaurs died out millions of years ago. The ancient alien theory says aliens made dinosaurs. They wanted to test life on Earth. Then the aliens killed them. They did this so people could live on Earth.

CHAPTER 2

HISTORY OF THE
Theory

Erich von Däniken is a Swiss writer. He believes this idea. He has looked for **proof** for more than 65 years.

He looks to religion. Many religions have a story. A being from the sky visits Earth. This being talks to people. It helps them. Some religions say that being was a god. Von Däniken says it was an alien.

Von Däniken believes
an alien came to Earth
as an astronaut in
ancient times.

Ancient alien believers think people did not learn how to make fire on their own. They think aliens taught them how to make fire.

Many believers say aliens are **advanced**. They say aliens gave people fire. Aliens shared their tools. Scientists disagree. They prove these ancient people made their own tools.

CHAPTER 3

ANCIENT ART

Ancient peoples made art. Some of their images look like aliens. Others look like people in flying ships. Believers say the drawings are of aliens. Scientists say the images are **symbols**. They show different stories.

Ancient alien believers think the Fremont people of Utah drew pictures of aliens in AD 1000.

NAZCA LINES

The Nazca lines are in Peru. More than 800 white lines are dug into the sand. Some are many miles long. They have hundreds of shapes. The lines can only be seen from the sky. How could people have made them?

Believers says aliens drew the lines. Scientists disagree. The top layer of rocks is dark. The Nazca people once cleared the rocks away. This showed the light sand underneath. They say this is how the shapes were made.

A view from above shows a tree drawing and a hand drawing in the Nazca lines.

ALIEN RUNWAYS

Believers also think the Nazca lines had a purpose. They think the lines were runways for alien spacecrafts.

EGYPTIAN LIGHT BULB

One Egyptian carving looks like a light bulb. The base is a flower. The "wire" inside is a snake. Scientists say the carving shows a **creation** story. Believers disagree. They say aliens gave the Egyptians electricity.

People disagree about what the ancient Egyptian carving that looks like a light bulb actually shows.

Ancient Egyptian art often used many birds. They represented life and death.

SAQQARA BIRD

The Saqqara Bird is a small wooden carved bird. It is about 2,200 years old. It looks like an airplane. Believers say aliens flew in ancient Egypt. They gave the Egyptians airplanes. The bird is a model of those airplanes. But scientists think the bird was a toy.

CHAPTER 4

ANCIENT
Buildings

Ancient alien believers look at old buildings. They say people could not have built them. The buildings are too big. They are too heavy. People did not have the right tools. Believers think aliens must have built them instead.

Puma Punku is an ancient temple in Bolivia that was made with advanced tools. Ancient alien believers think aliens provided the tools.

Thousands of workers built the pyramids.

PYRAMIDS

The Great Pyramid is more than 4,500 years old. It is made of millions of stone blocks. Each block weighs between 2 and 15 tons. How did people move the blocks? How did they fit them into place?

Believers say aliens did it. Scientists disagree. They say people moved the blocks on wooden sleds. They used copper tools. Scientists have found these tools.

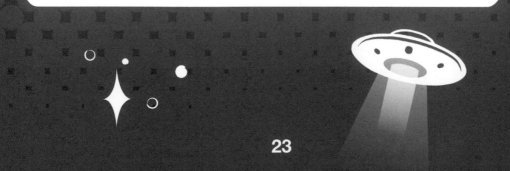

EASTER ISLAND

About 900 stone heads stand on Easter Island. They are huge. Each one is about 13 feet (4 meters) tall. Each weighs 14 tons. They are more than 1,000 years old. Believers say people could not have made them. Aliens did the work. Scientists disagree. They say the Rapa Nui people built the heads. They moved the heads using ropes.

The Easter Island heads are called Moai. They were built between 1250 and 1500 BC.

Ancient alien believers think aliens helped build the pyramids and so much more.

The theory says people needed aliens. They gave people new tools and skills. Scientists say ancient peoples could accomplish many things. What do you think?

GLOSSARY

advanced
further along in terms of progress of development

alien
referring to life from outer space

ancient
very old

creation
the process of bringing something new into existence

proof
the facts showing that something is true

symbol
an image or idea used to represent something else

theory
an idea meant to explain something

TRIVIA

1. Akhenaten was an Egyptian ruler. Images of him show a long head and long neck. Some people say he could have been an alien.

2. Pakal was a Mayan king. An image seems to show him in a spaceship. Scientists say these images are part of a Mayan myth. They think the image that looks like a spaceship is actually the Mayan sun god. The image shows Pakal riding into the underworld. The underworld was where the sun went at night.

3. The Puma Punku temple in Bolivia is made of many stones. Many of them weigh more than 110 tons. Some ancient alien believers do not think humans could have moved them alone. They think aliens helped move the stones.

ACTIVITY

BELIEVERS VS. SCIENTISTS

Alien theory believers give many examples of aliens helping ancient humans. Scientists disagree that aliens ever visited Earth. Choose one of the building examples in this book. Research the example online. Then write a paragraph arguing from a believer's point of view. Why must aliens have been involved? Why couldn't humans have built the structure themselves? Next write a paragraph arguing from a scientist's point of view. What tools could ancient humans have used to build the structure? What evidence do people have today?

FURTHER RESOURCES

Want to know more about aliens? Learn more here:

Martin, Michael. *The Unsolved Mystery of Alien Abductions.* North Mankato, Minn.: Capstone Press, 2014.

PBS Learning Media: Is It Irrational to Believe in Aliens?
https://tpt.pbslearningmedia.org/resource/is-it-irrational-pbs-space-time/is-it-irrational-pbs-space-time/

Curious about the science behind aliens? Check out these websites:

PBS Learning Media: How to Signal Aliens
https://tpt.pbslearningmedia.org/resource/how-to-signal-pbs-space-time/how-to-signal-pbs-space-time/

PBS Learning Media: Why Haven't We Found Alien Life?
https://tpt.pbslearningmedia.org/resource/why-havent-we-found-pbs-space-time/why-havent-we-found-pbs-space-time

INDEX